Temple Architecture in India

(B. K. Das)

(Reference Hand book)

Preface

This short handbook of Temple Architecture in India is meant for non Indian readers who want to understand the basic philosophy of Indian Hindu Temple. The contents are in brief and simple language avoiding Sanskrit jargons for better understanding. Content of this reference book is from multiple sources including the internet.

Contents

1. Religion and Temple

Great religions on Indian Sub continent and their main God.

Hinduism- Brahma, Vishnu and Mahesh

Buddhism- Lord Buddha

Jainism- Mahavira

Sikhism- Guru Govind Singh

Hinduism is the oldest religion of the world dating back to 2000 BCE. The first resemblance of Lord Shiva is from Indus Valley Civilization (2500 BC) with the archaeological finding of seal of 'Pashupati'.

A Hindu temple is a symbolic house, seat and body of god. It is a structure designed to bring human beings and gods together, using symbolism to express the ideas and beliefs of Hinduism.[2][3] The symbolism and structure of a Hindu temple are rooted in Vedic traditions, deploying circles and squares. A temple incorporates all elements of Hindu cosmos—presenting the good, the evil and the human, as well as the elements of Hindu sense of cyclic time and the essence of life—symbolically presenting *dharma, kama, artha, moksa,* and *karma*

1

2. Temples Styles of India

Three temple styles developed in India.

1. *Nagara* style

2. *Dravidian* style

3. *Visera* style

Nagara style was commonly known as North Indian Style and it stretched from Himalyan range to Vindhyas.

Dravidian style commonly known as South Indian Style and it stretched from River Krishna to whole of South India.

Apart from this a confluence of North and South Indian style seems to fuse together at a location in Karnataka state of India. This style is known as *Visera* style. It ranges from Vindhyas to River Krishna.

So, Indian temple architecture is classified by some historian into three distinct styles.

3. Aspects in Temple Construction

Construction of a temple was always considered a sacred activity. The timely completion of these Abodes, along with attention to the minutest details, required strict hierarchy of commands. On top of the hierarchy was the person who dreamt of a temple for his *isht (*God*)*. He was *Yajmana /Karta* or the Patron. Most of the time, *Yajmana* was a king, a queen or a rich businessman and used to choose the *Mukhya Sthapatyapati* or the Chief Architect. *Mukhya Sthapatyapati* was expected to be the master of *Shilpa Shastra, Vaastu Shastra, Dharma Shastra, Agnipurana* and all mathematical calculations. He was the person responsible for converting *Karta's* dream into an architectural draft.

He was empowered to select his chief engineer, the *Sutra Grahini,* who was responsible for converting the architectural draft into geometrical design and dimensions. In order to avoid confrontations, ego clashes and to work in perfect synchronization, *Sutra Grahini* was usually the son of *Mukhya*

Sthapatyapati. They were assisted in their task by *Murtikar* the sculptor), *Sangatarash* (the mason) and the painter. These were the senior technical specialists who then commanded many others to get the job done.

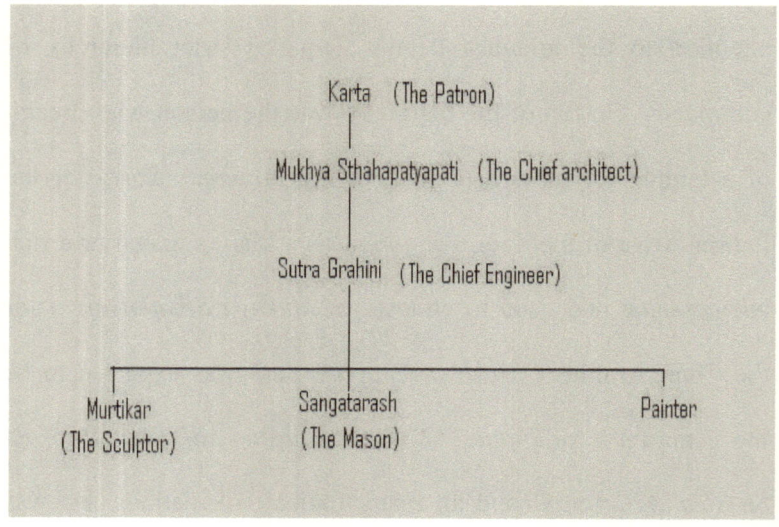

Temple construction begins with search of a proper site (site selection). Soil and location are examined by *acharya* and *shilpi*. This is called *Bhupariksha* (land examination)

This is followed by *nagara/grama* (town/village) nirmana. Here, the layout of town, its size, breadth of different levels of streets, locations and sizes of facilities like water tanks are determined based on the size of town (site planning). There are different names for different sizes of towns, like *grama, kheta, kharvata, durga, nagara.* Then the location of temple (brahma sthana) in the town is decided. Temple is usually in the center of village so that every villager has access to it (irrespective of caste). The entire arrangement is called *grama vinyasa.*

Then the size of temple is determined. For this, size of the image of main deity is to be known, since the size of a temple is always a fixed multiple of the size of image of main deity (proportion). Then wood/metal/stone is selected for the image. The icon has three parts, main icon (*vigraha*), pedestal (*peetha*) and platform (*adhisthana or upa peetha*). The tests to determine quality of stone are prescribed by the *Agamas.* There are three kinds of stone, male female and neuter. When hit with an iron rod if the stone produces good sound and spark, it is male and should be used for the main deity or icon. If it produces sound but not spark it is female and should be used for pedestal. If it produces neither, it is neuter and should be used for platform. There are various standards for the relative proportions of image, *gopura,*

5

prakara etc. and also the relative proportions of various parts of the *vigraha*. The units for measuring *vigraha* are *tala, angula* and *yava*. Tala is a multiple of *angula* and *angula* is a multiple of *yava*. More than the specific size of each unit, the multiplicity and relative sizes are important. The proportions of Head-Trunk-Arms-Legs of images are specified. The finer specifications like nose, nail, ears and their shapes are also mentioned. Generally the standard is to use *dasatala* (ten talas) for the height of image of male deity, *navatala* (nine talas) for His consort and *astatala* (eight talas) for *bhakta*.

Duties of temple administration are also specified in the *Agamas* - organizing festivals, encourage art forms and conduct shows to encourage artists, create accommodation for pilgrims from other towns, run hospitals, regularly conducting religious discourses etc.

Town planning, engineering, architecture, fine arts, civics, and many other subjects are dealt in the *agamas*, which relate to the various interests of people and involve them at different capacities and also direct their work towards a higher goal.

Steps in Temple Construction

The procedure for building a temple is extensively discussed, and it could be expressed in short as "*Karshanadi Pratisthantam*", meaning beginning with "*Karshana*" and ending with "*Pratistha*". The details of steps involved vary from one Agama to another, but broadly these are the steps in temple construction:

***Bhu pariksha* (land survey and soil testing)**: Examining and choosing location and soil for temple and town. The land should be fertile and be able to support the habitation.

Sila pariksha: Examining and choosing material for image

Karshana: Corn or some other crop is grown in the place first and is fed to cows. Then the location is fit for town/temple construction.

Vastu puja: Ritual to propitiate vastu devata.

Salyodhara: Undesired things like bones are dug out.

Adyestaka: Laying down the first stone

*Nirmana (*construction*):* Then foundation is laid and land is purified by sprinkling water. A pit is dug, water mixed with *navaratnas, navadhanyas, navakhanijas* is then put in and pit is filled. Then the temple is constructed.

Murdhestaka sthapana: Placing the top stone over the prakara, gopura etc. This again involves creating cavities filled with gems minerals seeds etc. and then the pinnacles are placed.

Garbhanyasa: A pot made of five metals (*pancaloha kalasa sthapana*) is installed at the place of main deity.

Sthapana: Then the main deity is installed.

Pratistha: The main deity is then charged with life/god-ness.

Before the temple is opened for daily worship, there are some preparatory rituals to be done, like:

Anujna: the priest takes permission from devotees and lord Ganesha to begin rituals

Mrit samgrahana: Collecting mud

Ankurarpana: Sowing seeds in pots of mud collected and waiting till they germinate

Rakshabandhana: The priest binds a holy thread on his hand to take up the assignment.

Punyahavacana: Purifying ritual for the place and invoking good omens

Grama santi: Worship for the good of village and to remove subtle undesired elements

Pravesa bali: Propitiation of various gods at different places in the temple, *rakshoghna puja* [to destroy *asuric* (demon)elements] and of specific gods like *Kshetra palaka* (*God* ruling the town)

Vastu Santi: Pacifying puja for vastu (this happens twice and this is the second time)

Yagasala: Building the stage for homas, along with vedika.

Kalasasthapana: Installing kalasam

Samskara: Purifying the yaga sala

9

Kalasa puja, yagarambha: Woshipping the kalasa as god and propitiating deities through fire

Nayanonmeelana, Pratimadhivasa: Opening eyes of the god-image, installing it and giving it life.

Then specific worship is done to deity, as prescribed. For instance in the case of Siva, this is followed by astabandhana and kumbhabhisheka.

Temple Design

From the proportions of the inner sanctum to the motifs carved into the pillars, the traditional temple takes its first form on the master sthapati's (architect) drawing board. The architect initially determines the fundamental unit of measurement using a formula called *ayadhi*. This formula, which comes from *Jyotisha,* or Vedic astrology, uses the nakshatra (birth star) of the founder, the nakshatra of the village in which the temple is being erected matching the first syllable of the name of the village with the seed sounds mystically associated with each *nakshatra* and the *nakshatra* of the main Deity of the temple. This measurement, called *danda*, is the dimension of the inside of the sanctum and the distance between the pillars. The whole space of the temple is defined in multiples and fractions of this basic unit.

The Shastras are strict about the use of metals, such as iron in the temple structure because iron is mystically the crudest, most impure of metals. The presence of iron, sthapatis (architect) explain, could attract lower, impure forces. Only gold, silver, and copper are used in the structure, so that only the most sublime forces are invoked during the *pujas*. At significant stages in the temple construction (such as ground-digging for foundation and placement of the *garbh griha* (sanctum) door frame, small pieces of gold, silver and copper (not iron) as well as precious gems, are ceremoniously embedded in small intersections between the stones, adding to the temple's inner-world magnetism. These elements (precious metals and stones) are said to glow in the inner cosmic worlds and, like holy ash, are prominently visible to the Gods and *Devas*.

The ground plan represents a symbolic cosmos miniature in scale. It is based on a strict grid made up of squares and

11

equilateral triangles which are imbibed with deep religious significance. To the priest-architect the square was an absolute and mystical form. The grid, usually of 64 or 81 squares, is in fact a *mandala*, a model of the cosmos, with each square belonging to a deity with its power and symbolic representation. The position of the squares on the mandala is in accordance with the importance attached to each of the deities, with the square in the center representing the temple deity the *brahmasthan* ; the outer squares cover the gods of lower rank. Agamas say that the temple architecture is similar to a man sitting - and the idol in garbagriha is exactly the heart-plexus, gopuram as the crown etc.

The construction of the temple follows in three dimensional form exactly the pattern laid out by the mandala. The relationship between the underlying symbolic order and the actual physical appearance of the temple can best be understood by seeing it from above which was of course impossible for humans until quite recently.

Another important aspect of the design of the ground plan is that it is intended to lead from the temporal (having finite life) world to the eternal (infinite). The principal shrine should face the rising sun and so should have its entrance to the east. Movement towards the sanctuary, along the east-west axis and through a series of increasingly sacred spaces is of great importance and is reflected in the architecture. A typical temple consists of the following major elements an entrance, often with a porch one or more attached or detached mandapas or halls the inner sanctum called the garbagriha, literally 'womb chamber' the tower build directly above the garbagriha.

Significance of the number eight in temple design

Vastu Shastra describes the inner sanctum and main tower as a human form, structurally conceived in human proportions based on the mystical number eight. The vibration of the space-consciousness, which is called time, is the creative element, since it is this vibratory force that causes the energetic space to turn into spatial forms. Therefore, time is said to be the primordial element for the creation of the entire universe and all its material forms. When these vibrations occur rhythmically, the resultant product will be an orderly spatial form. This rhythm of the time unit is traditionally called *talam* or *layam.*

Since every unit of time vibration produces a corresponding unit of space measure, *vastu* science derives that time is equal to space. This rhythm of time and space vibrations is quantified as eight and multiples of eight, the fundamental and universal unit of measure in the vastu silpa tradition. This theory carries over to the fundamental *adi talam* (eight beats) of classical Indian music and dance. Applying this in the creation of a human form, it is found that a human form is also composed of rhythmic spatial units. According to the Vastu Shastras, at the subtle level the human form is a structure of eight spatial units devoid of the minor parts like the hair, neck, kneecap and feet, each of which measures one-quarter of the basic measure of the body and, when added on to the body's eight units, increases the height of the total form to nine units. Traditionally these nine units are applied in making sculptures of Gods.

Since the subtle space within our body is part of universal space, it is logical to say that the *talam* of our inner space should be the same as that of the universe. But in reality, it is very rare to find this consonance between an individual's and the universal rhythm. When this consonance occurs, the person is in harmony with the Universal Being and enjoys spiritual strength, peace and bliss. Therefore, when designing a building according to *vastu*, the architect aims at creating a space that will elevate the vibration of the individual to resonate with the vibration of the built space, which in turn is in tune with universal space. *Vastu* architecture transmutes the individual rhythm of the indweller to the rhythm of the Universal Being.

The Vastu-Purusha-Mandala

The goal of a temple's design is to bring about the descent or manifestation of the unmanifest and unseen. The architect or sthapati begins by drafting a square. The square is considered to be a fundamental form. It presupposes the circle and results from it. Expanding energy shapes the circle from the center; it is established in the shape of the square. The circle and curve belong to life in its growth and movement. The square is the mark of order, the finality to the expanding life, life's form and

15

the perfection beyond life and death. From the square all requisite forms can be derived: the triangle, hexagon, octagon, circle etc. The architect calls this square the *vastu-purusha-mandala-vastu*, the manifest, *purusha*, the Cosmic Being, and *mandala*.

The *vastu-purusha-mandala* represents the manifest form of the Cosmic Being; upon which the temple is built and in whom the temple rests. The temple is situated in Him, comes from Him, and is a manifestation of Him. The *vastu-purusha-mandala* is both the body of the Cosmic Being and a bodily device by which those who have the requisite knowledge attain the best results in temple building. *Vastu* refers the physical environment, *Purusha* refers to energy, power, cosmic being and *Mandala* being diagram or charts.

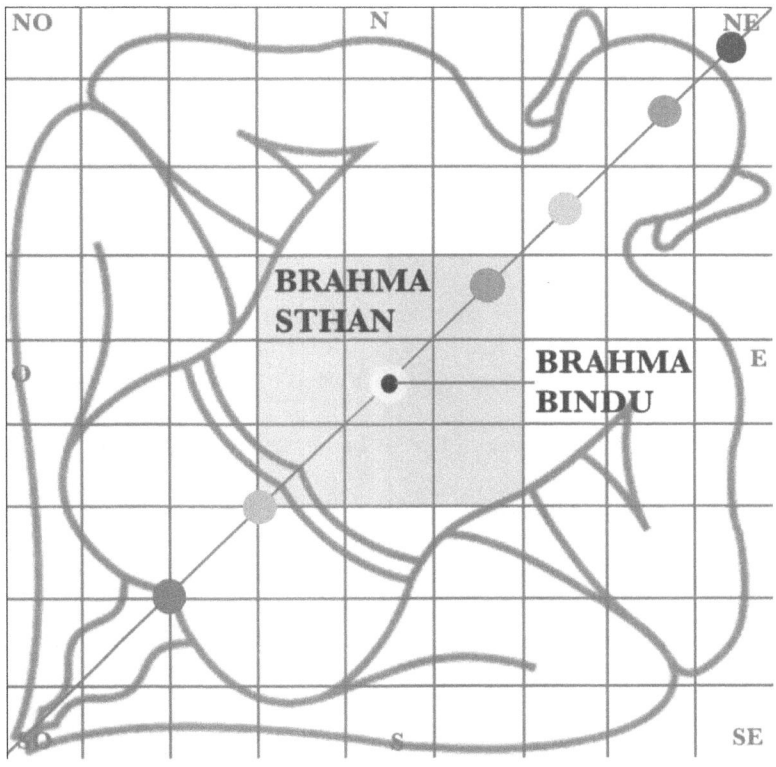

Fig. No.1 Vastu Purush Mandala

In order to establish the *vastu-purusha-mandala* on a construction site, it is first drafted on planning sheets and later drawn upon the earth at the actual building site. The drawing of the *mandala* upon the earth at the commencement of construction is a sacred rite. The rites and execution of the *vastu-*

17

purusha-mandala sustain the temple in a manner similar to how the physical foundation supports the weight of the building.

Based on astrological calculations the border of the *vastu-purusha-mandala* is subdivided into thirty-two smaller squares called *nakshatras*. The number thirty-two geometrically results from a repeated division of the border of the single square. It denotes four times the eight positions in space: north, east, south, west, and their intermediate points. The closed polygon of thirty-two squares symbolizes the recurrent cycles of time as calculated by the movements of the moon. Each of the nakshatras is ruled over by a Deva, which extends its influence to the mandala. Outside the mandala lie the four directions, symbolic of the meeting of heaven and earth and also represent the ecliptic of the sun-east to west and its rotation to the northern and southern hemispheres.

4. Temple Elements

Every Hindu temple should face towards East direction. It is believed that the ray of the rising Sun must penetrate the temple interior and shine the chief diety housed in *garbh griha.*

Garbh Griha

Garbh Griha, is the main part of the temple where the God or symbolism of God is placed. It is either square in Plan or Rectangular. Male God is housed in square garbh griha and female Goddess in rectangular garbh griha. The circumambulation passage around *girbhgrih* is known as *Pradakshina*. However, not all temples have *pradakshina*; a temple without an ambulatory passage is known as *Nirandhara-prasada*. Some of the large temples have subsidiary shrines on the four corners of the complex. They are known as *Panchayatna* or five-shrine temple complex.

Mandapas

Before entering the garbh griha there are series of spaces in different temples. These are the transition spaces through which devotees enter.

Shikhara /Vimana

Vimana is the pyramidal projection above the Garbh Griha which gives elevation to the temple.

Amalaka

It is disc like structure at the top of Vimana

Kalasha

It is the water vessel above amalaka and is the top most part of a temple.

Antarala

This area is transition between Garbh griha and mantapa (temples main hall). At the time of prayer devotees assemble here.

Jagati

It is the raised platform for sitting and praying for the devotees.

Vahana

It is the vehicle or mount of the main deity placed axially the garbh griha

Water

A water body in the form of river, lake or pool is essential component of Hindu Temple.

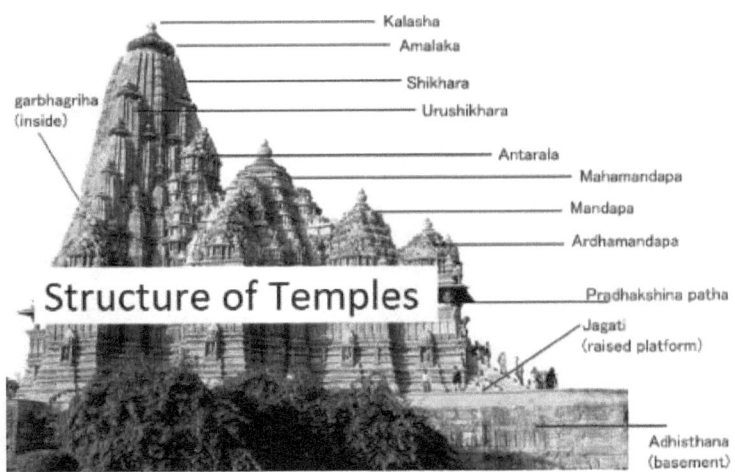

Fig. No.2 Elements of Temple

21

5. North Indian Style (Nagara style)

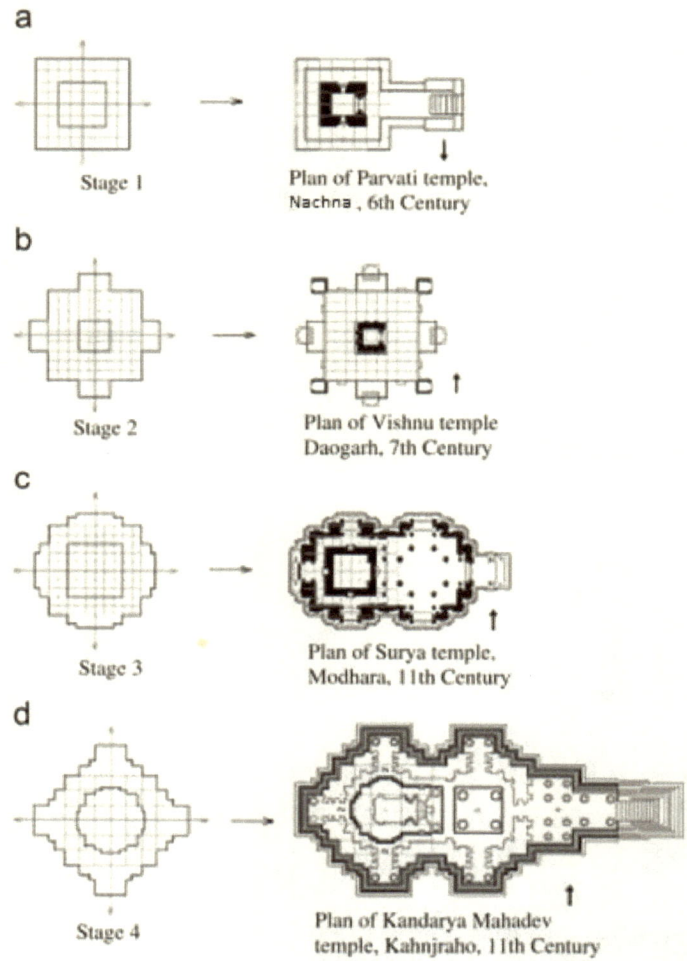

a

Stage 1

Plan of Parvati temple,
Nachna , 6th Century

b

Stage 2

Plan of Vishnu temple
Daogarh, 7th Century

c

Stage 3

Plan of Surya temple,
Modhara, 11th Century

d

Stage 4

Plan of Kandarya Mahadev
temple, Kahnjraho, 11th Century

Fig. No. 3 Chronological evolution of temple in North India.

(a) Parvati temple, Nachna from simple square *mandala (c.a. 4th*
Century A.D.)

Fig. No.4 Parvati Temple, Nachna, Madhya Pradesh

Parvati Temple is dedicated to the goddess **Parvati**, consort of
Shiva. This structure is one of the monument among Khajuraho
Group of Monuments, a World Heritage Site in India. the oldest
temple of India and it is a previous architecture of Gupta art. The
figures on the outer walls and on the doorway have the figures of the
Ganges and Jamuna standing on their respective symbols, the
crocodile and tortoise. All the roofs are flat, like those of known
Gupta temples.

It is a building of two stories. It is nearly square, 15'9" by 15' with
plain perpendicular walls. The lower storey is surrounded by a

roofed cloister upwards of 5' wide which is closed. In front of the entrance there is an open, unroofed court, nearly 12' square, which is reached by flight steps, 4½' in height.

The upper story is quite plain both inside and outside. It is covered by a flat roof of apparently three slabs. These are still on the top of the wall, but are much tiled and out of position. The doorway is on the west, and the chamber is lighted by two trellises, one in each side wall. These are formed simply by two plain loop holes, one on each side.

The doorway of the lower storey is very richly carved with human figures in pairs on each jamb, ending with small statues of the Ganges and Yamuna. There are no obscene figures. The sanctum is dimly lighted on each side by a stout trellis of simple square holes, which receives its light from another trellis in the cloister wall opposite. In the middle of each of the outer faces there is a large trellis, with two horned loins and two men. On one side the trellis has four small pillars, with three openings, each pillar being ornamented with a human figure.

The outer faces of the wall (expecting only the upper room) are carved to imitate rock work. A few figures are introduces, as well as a few lions or bears lying in holes or caves in the rock-work.

(b) Vishnu temple (Dashavatara), Deogarh, Lalitpur district, Uttar Pradesh- from the first iteration of *mandala.(6th century*

A.D.)

Fig. No. 5 View of Dashavatara temple

The Dashavatara Temple is an early 6th century Vishnu temple located at Deogarh, Uttar Pradesh in the Betwa River valley in north-central India. It has a simple, one cell square plan and is one of the earliest Hindu stone temples still surviving today.

(c) plan of Surya temple, Modhera from the second iteration of *mandala (11th Century A.D.)*

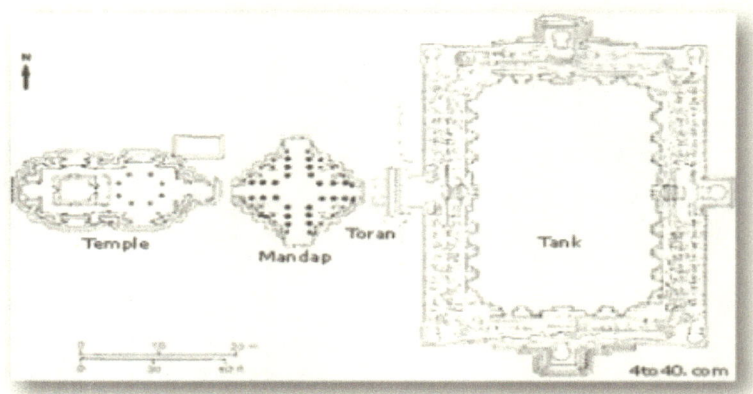

Fig. No. 6 Plan of Sun temple Modhera, Gujarat

The Sun temple complex is built in Maru-Gurjara style (Chaulukya style). The temple complex has three axially aligned components; the shrine proper (garbhagriha) in a hall (gudhamandapa), the outer or assembly hall (sabhamandapa or rangamandapa) and a sacred reservoir (kunda).The sabhamandapa is not in continuation with gudhamandapa but is placed little away as a separate structure. Both are built on paved platform. Their roofs have collapsed long ago leaving behind few lower-most courses. Both roofs are 15' 9" in diameter but are constructed differently. The platform or plinth is inverted lotus shaped.

Fi.g No. 7 View of stepped pool and Sun temple at Modhera.

(d) Kandarya Mahadev temple,Khajuraho from the third iteration of *mandala.(1030 A.D.)*

Kandariya Mahadeva is dedicated to God Shiva and is in Central India.

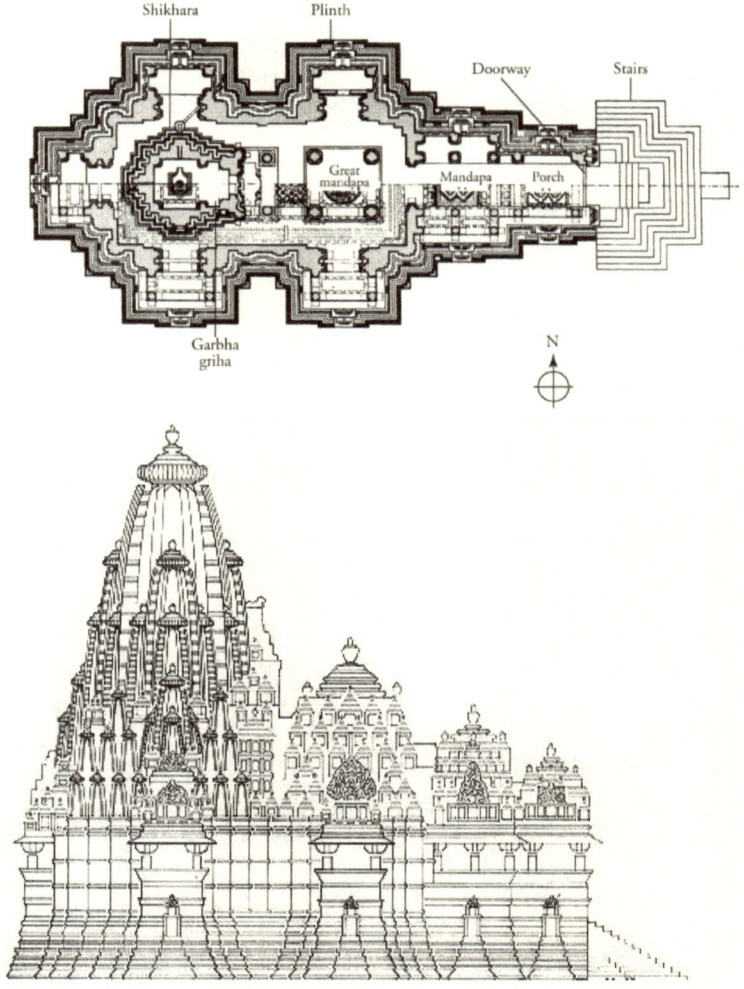

Fig. No. 9 Plan and Elevation of Kandarya Mahadeva, Khajuraho.

Temples of Orissa state in India.

Fig. No 10 Plan and elevation of Orissan style temple of Lingaraj

Sequence of entry in Orissan style temple is through Vogamandir (place of offering), Nattmandir (place of dance and music), Jagamohan (place of assembly) and the Garbh griha (the house of deity)

The elevation of jagamohana has horizontal lines as feature elements while the Vimana (over garbh griha) has vertical lines which gives optical illusion of greater height of vimana.

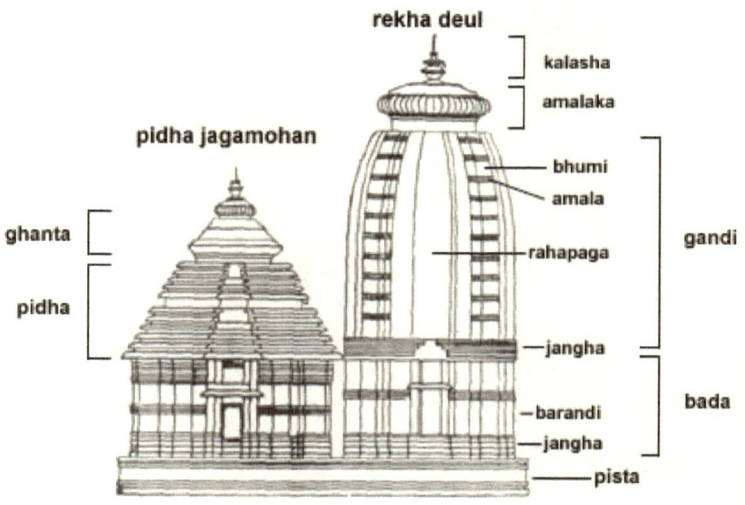

Fig. No. 11 Elevation of Lingraj Temple (jagmohan and Garbh griha

6. South Indian (Dravidian) style temples

The temples in horizontal plan represents God in sleeping position with *girbhgriha* as the *mastaka* and the *gopuram* (the gateways of South Indian temple architecture) forming the feet.

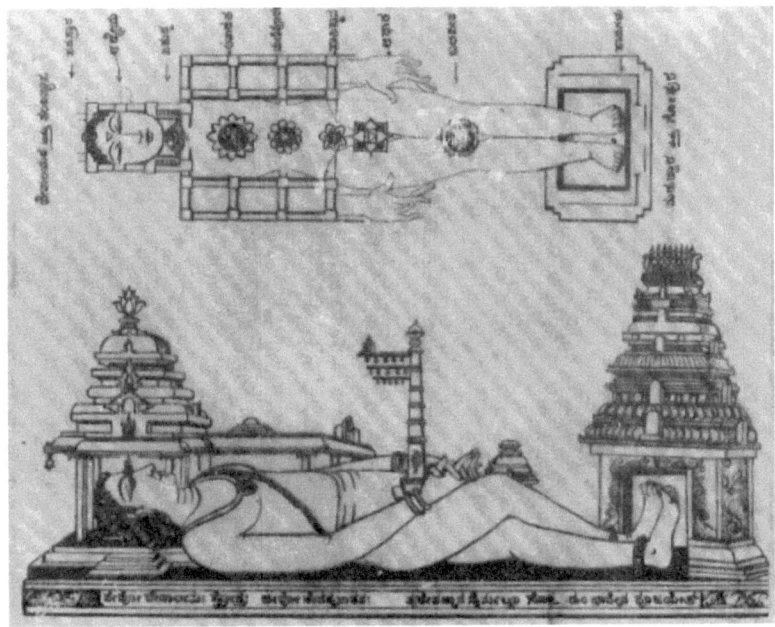

Fig. No. 12 Symbolic representation of South Indian Temple

It is believed that at many South Indian sites of religious antiquity the earlier buildings were not of great artistic taste. However, they held great sanctity because of deep and lasting veneration of enshrined idols. So, when the new and powerful dynasty like the Pandyas wanted to add something of their taste they ended making high walls and entrances to these enclosures into gateways of imposing size and appearances. Also the increase in rituals and the powers ascribed to the deities was also responsible for converting these structures into the palaces of Gods and Goddesses along with the homes of the attending, worshipping and caretaking Brahmins.

The enlargement of the southern temple proceeded on following lines: The shrine and its porch formed the innermost court with a small *gopuram* (gateway) at the entrance. In course of time, this covered court itself was contained into another court with two entrance *gopurams*. It was further enclosed by rectangular enclosures bounded by high walls. A wide open courtyard known as *Parakarm* was left all around. Within this *Parakarm* were added other structures, chiefly pillared halls and subsidiary shrines. There were also buildings of semi-religious characters like granaries and room for storing ceremonial supplies. This enclosure was also entered through two *gopurams*. After a time, a still higher enclosing wall added, leaving another larger *Parakaram* around. Within this last enclosure, two important structures were constructed, the hall of Thousand Pillars and a Tank for ceremonial bathing. Four *gopurams* led into this *prakaram* and each set was larger than the ones of the previous *parakaram*.

Almost invariably the two lower stories of the *gopuram* are vertical and are built of solid stones. It provided solid foundation for the super structure of lighter materials such as brick and plaster. The tower section is pyramidal in shape and is composed of a series of diminishing tiers in their ascend. The average angle of slope from the vertical is 25 degrees and width at the top is approximately half of its base.

Shore Temple, Mahabalipuram (700-728 A.D.)

Shore Temple overlooking Bay of Bengal was built in 700-728 AD with granite by the Pallava kingdom. Mahabalipuram was a port city and temple would have been the landmark for both the ships and the people on land.

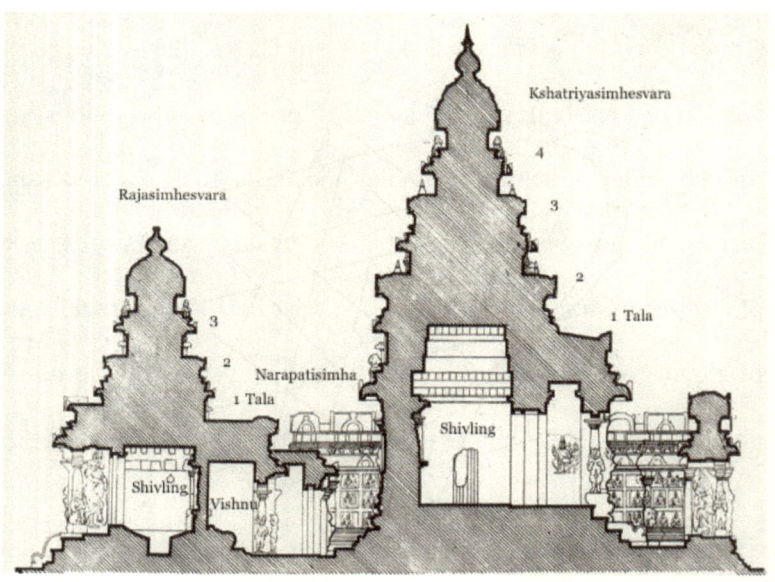

Fig. No. 13 Section of Shore temple.

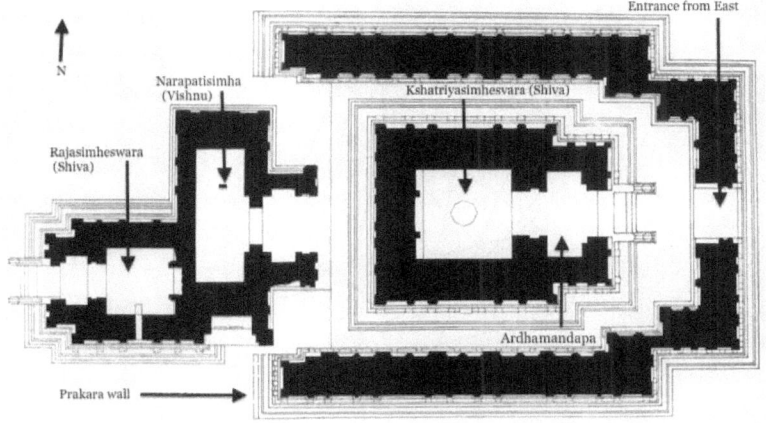

Fig. No.14 Plan of Shore temple.

Shore Temple is also acknowledged for being the first stone structure made by Pallavas. Before this, the monuments used to be carved out of the rocks or stones. Unlike other monuments of the region, Shore Temple is a five-storied rock-cut structural temple more willingly than monolithical. In southern India, this is one amongst the earliest and most important structural temples. The spire is extensively decorated with carvings and sculptures. In the recent years, a stone wall has been constructed to protect the shrine from further sea-erosion.

Perched on a 50 feet square plinth, the pyramidal structure raises to the extent of 60 feet. Presenting a typical specimen of Dravidian temple architecture, Shore Temple generates an exclusive combination of history and natural splendor. The temple was designed to grasp the first rays of the rising sun and to spotlight the waters after sunset. In the words of Percy Brown, Shore Temple served as "a landmark by day and a beacon by night".

Brihadeshwara Temple, Tanjavur, Tamil Nadu (1003-1010 AD)

Built by Chola dynasty, this granite temple is the tallest temple of South India. Dedicated to Lord Shiva

Fig. No. 15 Elevation of Brihadeshwara temple

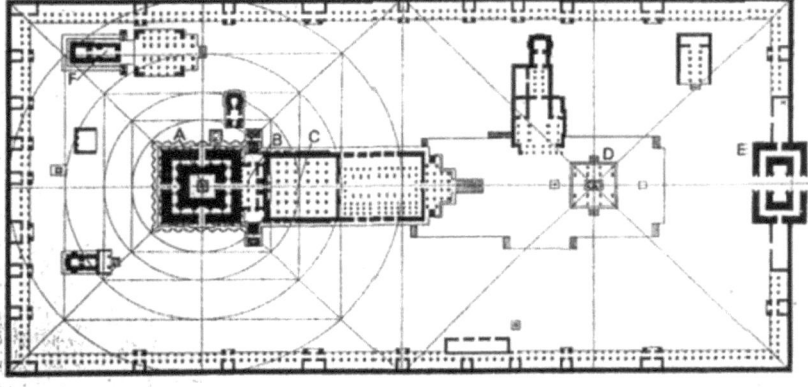

Fig. No. 16 Plan of Brihadeshwara temple

Meenakshi Temple, Madurai, Tamil Nadu

This temple is dedicated to Meenakshi, a form of Parvati, and Sundareswar, a form of Shiva. The temple is a fortified complex with walls all around measuring 258 m by 220 m. Present structure was built in 17th Century CE after the original temple was destroyed by Muslim general sent by Khilji ruler of Delhi.

Fig. No. 17 View of Meenakshi Temple

Temple is flanked by four *gopuram* (entrance gate) in all the four directions to enter the temple. Total eleven *gopurams* adorn the temple. Four main *gopurams* are 45 m in height and are carved with life size figure from Hindu mythology.

The sanctuary of Shiva has a assembly hall, a vestibule and a cella. The sanctuary of Meenakshi is half that of Shiva. Temple complex has a lily pool measuring 49.5 m by 36 m.

Fi.g No. 18 Painted sculpture of Gopuram

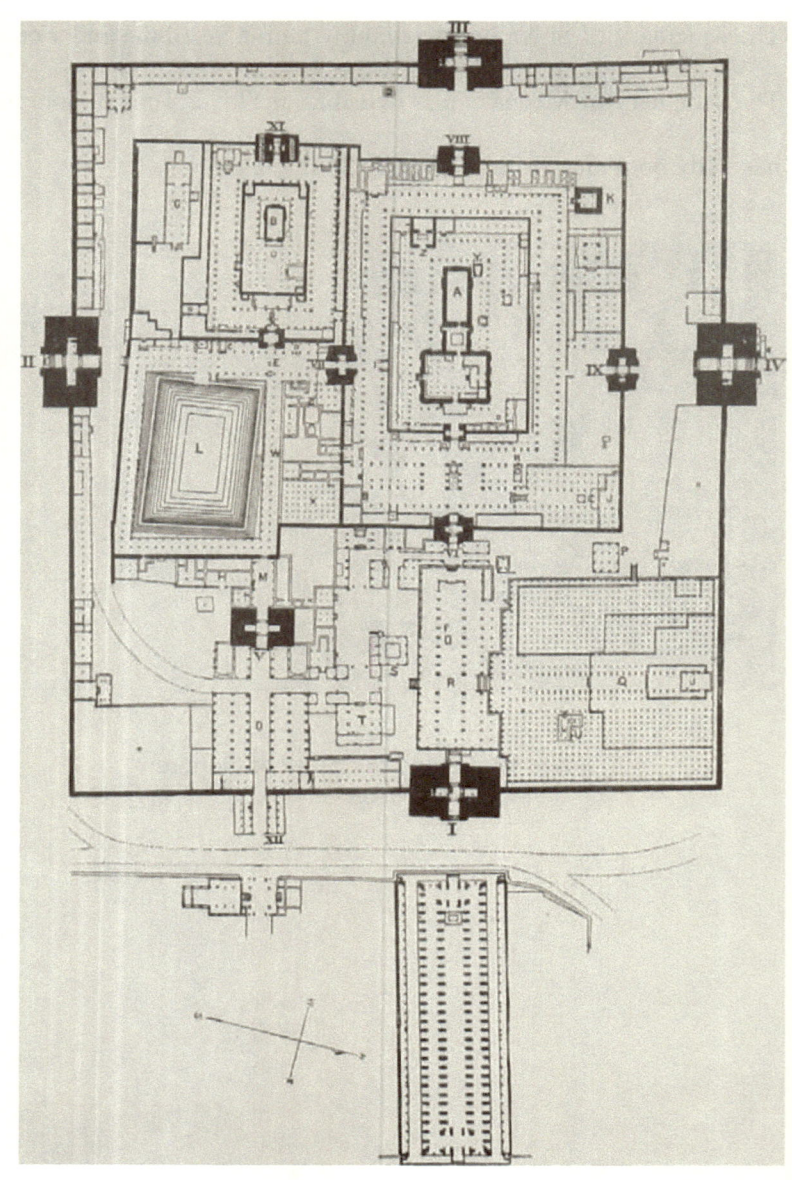

Fig. No. 19 Plan of Meenakshi Temple

40

7. Visera Style Temple

This style was adopted in the region that today lies in the modern states of Karnataka and Andhra Pradesh. True to their geographical position as buffer between north and south, this architectural style has mix of both the Nagara and Dravidian temple styles. These temples have *Shikhars* resembling Nagara temples and the rich carving style is apparently the influence of Dravidian temple architecture style. Vesara is also known as Hoysala architectural style and was promoted by Hoysala Kings who ruled over Mysore area from AD 1050 to AD 1300. Departing from Dravidian style it does not have covered ambulatory around the sanctum.

Example: Lad Khan temple at Aihole, Temples at Badami, Virupaksha temple – Pattadakal, Hoysala temples at Karnataka.

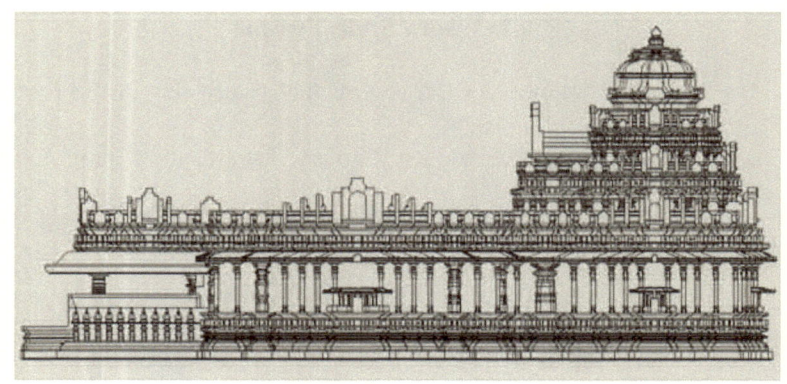

Fig. No. 20 Elevation of Virupaksha Temple at Pattadakal, Karnataka

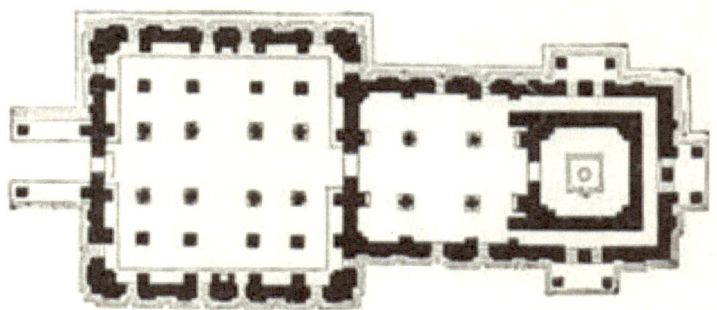

Fig Fig. No. 21 Plan of Virupaksha Temple at Pattadakal, Karnataka

Ladkhan Temple, Aihole : (7th-8th Century AD) Rashtrakuta dynasty.

Lad Khan temple: Consists of a shrine with two mantapas in front of it. The shrine bears a Shiva lingam. The mukha mantapa in front of the sanctum has a set of 12 carved pillars. The sabhamantapa in front of the mukha mantapa has pillars arranged in such a manner as to form two concentric squares. There are also stone grids on the wall carrying floral designs. The temple is built in a Panchayat hall style, indicating a very early experiment in temple construction. The windows are filled with lattice style which is a north Indian style. The temple was built in late 7th or early 8th century.

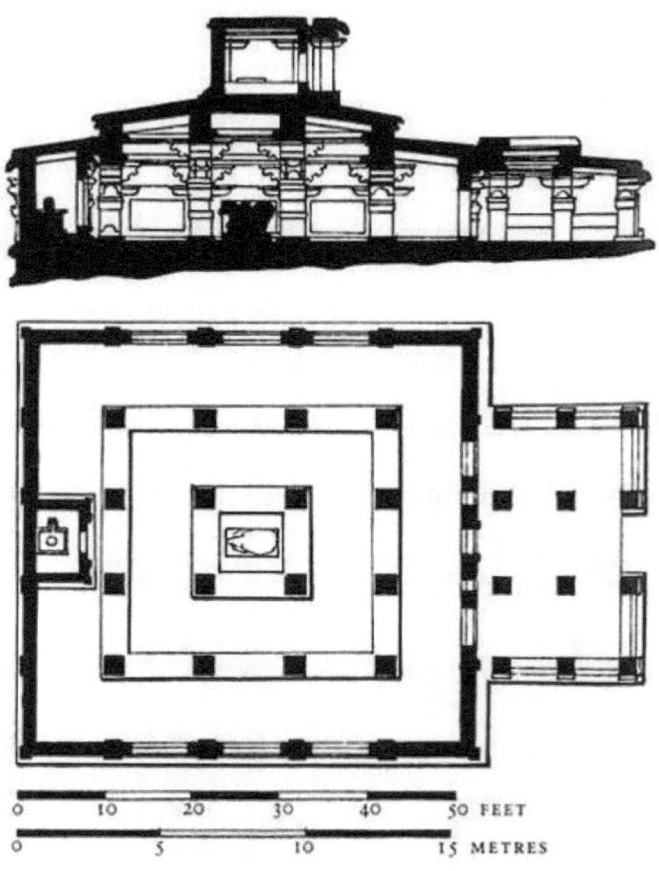

Fig. No.22 Section and Plan of Ladkhan temple at Aihole

44

8. Other Temples

Kailash Temple:

This temple located at Ellora village in Aurangabad, Maharashtra is rock cut temple and is the most magnificent work ever done by Humans in shaping the mountain to give a temple form.

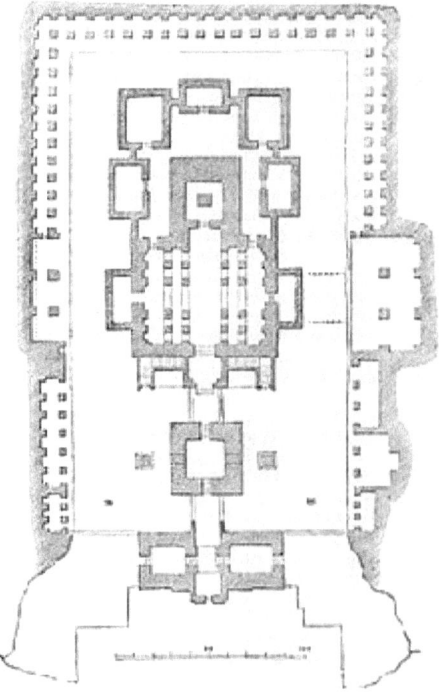

Fig. No.23 Plan of Kailash temple Ellora

The entrance to the temple courtyard features a low gopuram. Most of the deities at the left of the entrance are Shaivaite (followers of Lord Shiva) while on the right hand side the deities are Vaishnavaites (followers of Lord Vishnu). A two-storeyed gateway

45

opens to reveal a U-shaped courtyard. The dimensions of the courtyard are 82 m x 46 m at the base. The courtyard is edged by a columned arcade three stories high. The arcades are punctuated by huge sculpted panels, and alcoves containing enormous sculptures of a variety of deities. Originally flying bridges of stone connected these galleries to central temple structures, but these have fallen.

Within the courtyard, there is a central shrine dedicated to Shiva, and an image of his mount Nandi (the sacred bull). The central shrine housing the *lingam* features a flat-roofed *mandapa* supported by 16 pillars, and a Dravidian *shikhara*. The shrine – complete with pillars, windows, inner and outer rooms, gathering halls, and an enormous stone *lingam* at its heart – is carved with niches, plasters, windows as well as images of deities, *mithunas* (erotic male and female figures) and other figures. As is traditional in Shiva temples, Nandi sits on a porch in front of the central temple. The *Nandi mandapa* and main Shiva temple are each about 7 metres high, and built on two storeys. The lower stories of the Nandi Mandapa are both solid structures, decorated with elaborate illustrative carvings. The base of the temple has been carved to suggest that elephants are holding the structure aloft. A rock bridge connects the *Nandi*

Mandapa to the porch of the temple. The base of the temple hall features scenes from Mahabharata and Ramayana.

Fig. No. 24 View of Kailash temple from Hill top

www.ingramcontent.com/pod-product-compliance
Lightning Source LLC
Chambersburg PA
CBHW050343290526
45785CB00006B/2608